Kim Vahnenbruck

Fictions of New York

The City as Metaphor in Selected American Texts

Anchor Academic
Publishing

Vahnenbruck, Kim: Fictions of New York: The City as Metaphor in Selected American Texts.
Hamburg, Diplomica Verlag GmbH 2012

ISBN: 978-3-95489-032-3
Print: Anchor Academic Publishing, an Imprint of Diplomica® Verlag GmbH, Hamburg, 2012

Bibliographical Information of the German National Library:
The German National Library lists this publication in the German National Bibliography.
Detailed bibliographic data can be found at: http://dnb.d-nb.de

The digital publication (eBook) of this work with the ISBN 978-3-95489-532-8 can be
purchased on the general market or directly from the publisher.

© Anchor Academic Publishing ein Imprint der Diplomica® Verlag GmbH
http://www.diplomica-verlag.de, Hamburg 2012
Printed in Germany

Contents

1 Introduction

> New York,
> Concrete jungle where dreams are made of,
> There's nothing you can't do,
> Now you're in New York,
> these streets will make you feel brand new,
> the lights will inspire you,
> lets hear it for New York, New York, New York[1]

These lines from the song *Empire State of Mind* (2009) by the famous American rapper, record producer and entrepreneur Jay-Z, who was born in Brooklyn, New York, reveal the challenge of capturing the City of New York in words or text. New York City is on the one hand celebrated as the place "where dreams are made of", whose "streets will make you feel brand new" and whose "lights will inspire you", but on the other hand also as a "[c]oncrete jungle".

The contrasting, yet at the same time very tempting ideas of the 'City that Never Sleeps' make it not only the most popular city in the United States, but also the most "dynamic, varied and perplexing in the world" (Gates ix). Robert A. Gates further describes the challenge for the writer, singer or song-writer: "There are no standards [one] can grasp; no guidelines [one] can follow", because [t]he City presents no standard language, philosophy, or neighborhood that can be labelled as typically New York" (ix).

In order to understand the city and its influences at least to some extent, it might be useful to talk about the name 'New York' and the events in history that helped to make it the most important and most famous city in the world.

When people talk about New York, the City of New York is referred to and more precisely the most densely populated borough of Manhattan. In 1898, the Bronx, Brooklyn, Manhattan, Queens and Staten Island were consolidated to the City of New York, which is part of the state of New York. Therefore, New York and New York City are almost always used synonymously and refer to the same part of the city: Manhattan. It can be subdivided into Lower, Midtown, and Uptown regions. Westbound the Hudson River divides the city from New Jersey and East Manhattan is separated from Long Island

---

[1] Jay-Z ft. Alicia Keys *Empire State of Mind*. http://www.magistrix.de/lyrics/Jay-Z%20ft.%20Alicia%20Keys/Empire-State-Of-Mind-405440.html. (February 25, 2011).

by the East River. Other frequently used nicknames are 'The Big Apple'[2], 'Gotham'[3], 'Center of the Universe', 'The City that Never Sleeps' and 'The Capital of the World'.

The city's history describes quite effectively why especially New York has inspired so much great writing and became famous for its literary variety and sheer volume. Phillip Lopate, in *Writing New York: A Literary Anthology*, summarizes the city's past as follows:

> From the start, the place was fast, boisterous, crowded, dirty, secular, and on the make. It began as a cosmopolitan, international port, a walking city with a vital street life and a housing shortage, and stayed that way. The more the metropolis grew, the more it attracted writers (Lopate XVII).

Yet, two incidents at the beginning of the nineteenth century helped New York to strengthen its identity and personality as a metropolis. One was the War of 1812, that changed America's self-opinion because then it could consider itself both politically and psychologically independent from Great Britain. This feeling also encouraged New York to "untie [its] provincial apron stings with British cities[4]"(Gates x). The second event was the completion of the Erie Canal during the early 1820s, which connected Lake Erie further west with New York and established it as the new and busiest mercantile center in the United States. "Post-Civil War prosperity and the opening of the West had encouraged massive waves of immigrants to seek success in the new world, and the first port-of-call for most was New York" (x). In the following years, the number of people immigrating to the United States and especially New York increased explosively[5].

---

[2]The term was coined by the sports journalist John Fitzgerald in the 1920s. It referred to the award, winner of the horse races around New York received.

[3]Washington Irving used Gotham City for New York in this essay collection *Salmagundi, or the Whims and Opinions of Launcelot Langstaff and Others* meaning "goat-town".

[4]British cities New York was always compared to were especially London and Liverpool, but also other European cities such as Paris.

[5]Figure no.1 shows this development and can be seen in the appendix at the end.

A result of the rise of the city's population was the establishment of ethnic neighborhoods and consequently also the rise of the first tenement slums, because many failed to pursue their dream of success in the new world. Poverty became a major aspect and created a polarized city "with clearly defined borders between the lifestyles and habitations of the rich and poor" (x).

Nevertheless, New York managed to save itself, because of its adaptability to new times and circumstances. Exactly this is represented in the great volume of different literature about the city of New York. For each author writing about the city, New York stands for something else. Consequently, making a proper choice with reference as to what novels should be analyzed was quite difficult. It serves as a metaphor and can be interpreted in various ways depending on the intention of writing, the author's experiences with the city and the living conditions of the characters within the story, because "the city often is part of the journey in the development of a protagonist [...]" (Sauter 37).

Therefore, this thesis wants to analyze how New York City is depicted and interpreted as a metaphor in selected American texts.

The first chapter (2 The City as a Metaphor) explains what a metaphor is, how the city has become one and serves as a basis for further analysis of the main part. The main part then gives different images of the city, starting with the novel by John Dos Passos which gives a panoramic overview of New York City between the 1890s and 1920s (chapter 3.1.1). In a second step, this work goes deeper into the city by analyzing the polarized neighborhoods of Edith Wharton and Stephen Crane (chapter 3.2.1) and their meaning for the protagonists. A third chapter is dedicated to Paul Auster who gives a very modern, metaphysical view on the city (chapter 3.3.1).

The thesis is summarized in form of the last chapter that tries to evaluate if the topography of New York plays an important role for the different meanings of the city.

2 The American City as Metaphor

Looking at the heading of this chapter, there are two words that need further explanation: This is first of all the word metaphor, then the American City with regards to its development, and finally the connection between the two.

Defining the term 'metaphor' offers an interesting insight into the topic. The term has its origin in Greek and means "carrying one place to another". It is a figure of speech and according to *The Concise Oxford Dictionary of Literary Terms* it makes a statement

> in which one thing, idea, or action is referred to by a word or expression normally denoting another thing, idea, or action, so as to suggest some common quality shared by the two [...] (Baldick 205).

The quote does not say anything about the quality of the metaphor itself, meaning if it shows negative or positive characteristics of the City. How most of the authors chosen for the thesis interpret New York will become clear in the following chapters.

The development of the use of the term 'metaphor' in connection to daily life can be traced back to Jeffersonian or even Crèvecoeurian times. America started out as a country that heavily depended on agriculture. Accordingly, Lester Roy Zipris points out that "[t]he seeds of the American Dream were sown in the soil of a rural society, but with the growth of immigration, technology, and industrialization, the nature of American society changed" (Zipris 3). Thomas Jefferson, American Founding Father, principal author of the Declaration of Independence and the third president of the young nation, was a great advocate of this way of life. In his work *Notes on the State of Virginia* (1785) he states "[t]hose who labour in the earth are the chosen people of God, [...]. The mobs of great cities add just so much to the support of pure government, as sores do to the strength of the human body" (Jefferson 164-165). He regarded cities as a burden to the American society because he was frightened that the young nation would increase their dependence on nations like Great Britain. It was his aim to support America to become independent politically and economically, which could only be achieved by the humble and virtuous cultivator.

Looking at the early years of the American society, one can aptly state that nature functioned as a metaphor for the people's place in life. This is supported by Zipris, who writes about J. Hector St. John de Crèvecoeur's *Letters from an American Farmer* (1783):

> [L]and, in his work, is no longer a symbol, as it was for the Puritans, but an emblem - a badge of one's citizenship rather than a sign of God's natural bounty. Land [...] [is] indicative, in a real and concrete way, of one's place in the daily life and world of one's community." (Zipris 8).

He introduced the ideal American citizen, the 'Yeoman', being in fact any man. By tilling the earth, the farmer will be able to gain citizenship in the democratic Republic and help fostering a simple, yet virtuous society.

Nevertheless, Jefferson soon had to accept cities as the centers of commerce and manufacturing because it would help the young nation to settle economically. He finally yielded: "'An equilibrium of agriculture, manufactures, and commerce, is certainly become essential to our independence'" (15). Still, he deeply distrusted life in the cities and already anticipated problems for the generations yet to come: vice, crime and poverty will be issues that the urban society will have to deal with.

Though, from then on the development of the cities could not be stopped anymore. "In the decade from 1860 to 1870, America's urban population increased only by about 9%; [...] During the fifty years from 1870 to 1920, the percentage of farm population declined steadily, sinking as low as 30.1% in 1920" (4). The transition from nature as a metaphor for life to the city as a metaphor was inevitable and so it became the new, "'generative frontier of ... growth and change'" (Hoffmann 401).

In 1978, Gerhard Hoffmann publishes his work *Raum, Situation, erzählte Wirklichkeit*, where he gives his reader further information on why the city became a metaphor for so many people at all:

> Hoffnung auf Verwirklichung des amerikanischen Traums von Glück, Erfolg und Freiheit in der großen, glänzenden Stadt [...]. Dieser plot der Queste macht die Stadt für die Literatur der Moderne, insbesondere für die moderne amerikanische Literatur und hier vor allem den amerikanischen Roman, zum Symbol, nicht nur zum Schauplatz und Milieu (401).

The city and especially New York City as the fastest growing and changing metropolis, now represents the American Dream. Irene Billeter Sauter points out that this is Manifest Destiny[6] since "[t]he United States have 'consistently defined [their] national identity through spatial models of expansion and ascension'" (Sauter 37).

Applying this to New York, one can say that the City is a perpetual motion machine, there is always movement, "it is always 'becoming'; it is not yet there yet nor will it ever be" (48). There is a constant physical change going on, new buildings are built and the infrastructure changes so that people can stay in motion. Furthermore, there is a constant change in the population of New York, for numerous immigrants arrive and look for a place to live and earn their living. These developments lead to certain urban characteristics that can be applied to New York: This is for once, the city's contradictory faces of glamour and misery and its man-made quality. Then, the gigantic built environment and the relative unimportance of nature. Additionally, what makes New York attractive or even the other way around is its offer of anonymity to the many as well as its large, dense population which provides space if not always the warmest of welcomes, for the immigrant. Typically New York is also its affable, loquacious working-class population speaking a streetwise vernacular, its fabled loneliness and alienation. Very important is its symbolic importance as the modern city par excellence and its addictive, temptress quality, which entraps newcomers and convince them - no matter how they may suffer at its hands - that no place else will do (cf. Lopate xvii-xix). This is what makes the city special and therefore also a metaphor for the life of the people living in New York.

Numerous writers have specifically dealt with the topic of the City as metaphor and one of them was Joachim von der Thüsen. He says that image-making of the city is governed by three linguistic operations: the symbolic, the metaphoric and the metonymic level (cf. von der Thüsen 2). For the sake of the argument, the symbolic and metonymic level are not considered here, but

---

[6]Manifest Destiny is the belief of the 19th century America that the United States are chosen by God to expand across the continent.

only the metaphoric one. He states that

> [o]n the metaphoric level of image-making, the city is expressed in terms of relatively concrete constructs and processes that have no overt connection to urban life. Thus the city is seen as body, monster, jungle, ocean or volcano (von der Thüsen 2).

That this is true shows on the one hand the quote of the song at the beginning of this work, where New York is described as a "concrete jungle", but on the other hand also several other literary works, such as Upton Sinclair's novel *The Jungle* (1906) or also the novels that will be discussed and analyzed in the following chapters. It will become obvious that the city cannot be understood as one metaphor, but must be seen as several metaphors, because "[t]here are as many cities as there are imaginations" (Weimer 6).

Another author who dealt with the city as a metaphor is David R. Weimer. He considered the question of reality within the stories, but he stresses that "most literary historians take [...] for granted - that the city is objectively real, [...]" (6). For many authors, such as Stephen Crane or Walt Whitman, it does not matter if the city is real, "but they wonder whether it is *solid*, which is to say prosaic, identifiable or unambiguous" (6). Thus, what really matters is that the city can be clearly identified as being typically New York, Boston or Chicago. In his novella *Maggie: A Girl of the Streets*, Stephen Crane does so by giving prominent street names or places that can only be found in New York City: "Pete, ranking his brains for amusement, discovered the Central Park Menagerie and the Museum of Arts" (Crane 36).

Therefore, one can summarize all the considerations on the city, the metaphor and their connection by quoting Weimer: "The 'city' of American literature is thus several cities, whose meaning and appeal derive first of all from their singularity" (Weimer 13). Nevertheless, one can assume that certain traits of the City can be found in each of the following novels since all the authors observe New York City in a time that was known and is still known for its rapid change and growth.

Exactly this can be discovered by taking a closer look at the various given pictures of New York by John Dos Passos, Stephen Crane, Edith Wharton and Paul Auster.

3 Pictures of New York City

3.1 Panorama of the City

3.1.1 John Dos Passos' *Manhattan Transfer*

John Roderigo Dos Passos (1898-1970) was considered to be a member of the so-called *Lost Generation*. This is a group of authors from the United States who came of age during World War I (1914-1918). According to the *Encyclopedia Britannica*,

> [t]he generation was 'lost' in the sense that its inherited values were no longer relevant in the postwar world and because of its spiritual alienation from a U.S. that, basking under Pres. Warren G. Harding's 'back to normalcy' policy, seemed to its members to be hopelessly provincial, materialistic, and emotionally barren. [7]

This generation of writers became disillusioned by the atrocities of the Great War and saw the development of greed, aggressiveness, corruption and capitalism with a very critical eye devolving to the cities of the United States, especially New York. A lot of these concerns and their consequences for society are worked up in their writings.

Furthermore, Dos Passos was one of the most important modernist writers in American literature. He made use of some very innovative novelistic techniques which, among others, are flashbacks, stream of consciousness or cinematic techniques. His impressionistic style [8] becomes evident throughout the novel by appealing to our senses with means of color, sound and smell.

The novel *Manhattan Transfer* was published in 1925 and was received as "'a novel of very first importance'" (Sinclair Lewis) (Passos Cover). Contrary to the plot, the novel is ironically clear structured. It comprises three sections which can be titled as 'arrival', 'stay' and 'farewell'. Each section again is separated into chapters, the first and last section having five and the

---

[7]Definition by the *Encyclopedia Britannica*: http://www.britannica.com/EBchecked/topic/348402/Lost-Generation (April 3, 2012).

[8]Impressionism is a rather vague term applied to works or passages that concentrate on the description of transitory mental impressions as felt by an observer, rather than on the explanation of their external causes (cf. Baldick 166-167).

middle section consisting of eight chapters. The smallest entity is the chapter itself, which can be structured as well. There is a headline, an epigraph and the text. From the headings of the several chapters one can deduce the topics of the novel, as will become clear in a later step.

Looking at the title of the novel, one can also draw conclusions as to what is important concerning structure, style as well as content. Matter of factly, Manhattan Transfer was a ferry connection on the Hudson River between New Jersey and New York City. The novel starts here, telling

> [g]ates fold upwards, feet step out across the crack, men and women press through the manuresmelling wooden tunnel of the ferryhouse, crushed and jostling like apples fed down a chute into a press (3)

and also ends "[o]ut [on] the empty dark fog of the river, [where] the ferryslip yawns all of a sudden, a black mouth with a throat of light" (342).

Taking a more careful look at the word "transfer", one gets the impression of motion and change. People transferring from the railroads to the ferries, a busy, pushing crowd of people. Everything is in motion, like a machine never willing to stop. This restless atmosphere can be discovered in every corner of New York City, because "in *Manhattan Transfer* the City continues to grow at a frantic pace; [...]. The birth of a megalopolis is on the horizon" (Gates 71). The changes in the City after the Great War were of both physical and mental nature. Industrialization and mechanization gave New York a whole new look, "creating concrete valleys of darkness during the day, and a dazzling display of lights at night" (64). The cityscape was now dominated by skyscrapers, such as the Lincoln Building or the Chrysler Tower. Many companies installed their headquarters in Manhattan and Gates further describes that "[n]ew roads were built as well as an extensive mass transit system that interconnected the separate Boroughs" (63). The growth and change is effectively described in the beginning of the by name fitting chapter *Metropolis*:

> His eyes fell on the headline on a *Journal* that lay on the floor by the coalscuttle where he had dropped it to run for the hack to take Susie to the hospital.
> MORTON SIGNS THE GREATER NEW YORK BILL
> COMPLETES THE ACT MAKING NEW YORK
> WORLD'S SECOND METROPOLIS (Passos 11).

9

There were also a lot of changes in the heads of the people living in the City. A fast increasing middle class that was hungry for setting themselves apart from the previous generation and achieving their own mores and ideals, created a new type of woman, "who considered herself totally liberated from the economic and social restrictions imposed upon her mother. She held jobs, wore shorter skirts, and bobbed her hair" (Gates 63). A higher affinity to organized crime and corruption could also be recorded during the post-war years, but was widely ignored until the stock market crash of 1929 made it all come to an end.

Though, not everyone saw this development being all positive. H.G. Wells observed that New York was becoming a "'steel-souled machine room', a city where 'individuals count for nothing ... the distinctive effect is the mass ... the unprecedented multitudinousness of the thing'" (65). This feeling is also noticeable in the novel of Dos Passos and so the intention of *Manhattan Transfer* is "to show the drift towards monopoly capitalism" (Gelfant, "John Dos Passos: The Synoptic Novel" 139) and its effects on society. It was not possible for the author to voice his criticism openly in the public, so he had to find a way doing it implicitly, "inherent in the picture of the times" (139). Dos Passos achieves this effect through various special techniques. Mrs. Gelfant aptly states: "The techniques that create the dramatic world of the novel establish toward it a firm social and moral attitude. Thus technique becomes the vehicle of social commentary" (141 f.). By analyzing the different stylistic means, it will become obvious in how far New York City serves as a metaphor in *Manhattan Transfer*.

A special trait of the novel is the "kaleidoscopic panorama of disparate scenes and characters that eventually collide with each other during the course of the plot" (Gates 71). This means, the author just gives a certain impression of reality. He does not give all the details and so achieves that the reader has to become active and complete the picture himself. The technique of abstraction helps Dos Passos to create the City as a place with a certain atmosphere and way of life embedded in its history. What becomes obvious is that *Manhattan Transfer* is not so much concerned with the people living in the City, but more with the development from the world's second metropolis to a mechanized, corrupted and alienated City. Thus, New York becomes the true protagonist of the novel and so justifies the heading of this thesis' chapter: *Panorama of the City*, for it provides the reader with an overview of the metropolis in a historical as well as social and economic sense. By abstracting the scenes presented in the novel and shifting from one to another quite often, something else is achieved: It "accelerates the novel's pace to suggest the incessant restless movement within the city itself" (Gelfant, "John Dos Passos: The Synoptic Novel" 143). So, the assumptions from the beginning, when the title of the novel was analyzed, is proved to be true.

Since John Dos Passos was known for his impressionistic streak, he proceeded his abstract technique through a distinctive use of colors. The first chapter of the novel concludes with a man buying a razor at "a yellowpained drugstore at the corner of Canal Street". Before, he walks up another East Side Street, "the sunstriped tunnel hung with skyblue and smokedsalmon and mustardyellow quilts, littered with second hand gingerbread-colored furniture" (Passos 9). The whole scene is just about one page long, a "fleeting sensuous impression" (Gelfant, "John Dos Passos: The Synoptic Novel" 143), but the dramatized use of the colors gives it "the quality of movement, so that abstracted colors 'agitate', 'flutter', and 'slide together'" (144). Seemingly static scenes become dynamic, because Dos Passos plays with light, shadow and color like a painter would (cf. Gelfant 144). An example is provided by a scene at a Mall at Central Park:

> She is walking [...] in the middle of great rosy and purple and pistachiogreen bubbles of twilight that swell out of the grass and trees and ponds, bulge against the tall houses sharp gray as dead teeth round the southern end of the park, melt into the indigo zenith (Passos 171).

The verbs "swell out", "bulge" and "melt" make the scene very dynamic, but they also exert a certain kind of pressure, which emanates from the great power the metropolis exerts on the individual. Gelfant concludes that "[t]he beauty of the city lies in its color formations, sometimes brilliant and gaudy, sometimes muted and subdued. All other sensory details, those of sound, weather, and odor, are oppressively ugly" (Gelfant, "John Dos Passos: The Synoptic Novel"

144).

Related to the statement given above by Gelfant, another technique of Dos Passos is the assault of the senses in general. Next to colors, he makes extensive use of addressing the reader's sense of hearing and smelling. Dos Passos has brilliantly brought the two sensory aspects together in one scene:

> The night was sultry. [...] The faraway sound of sirens from the river gave him gooseflesh. From the streets he heard footsteps, the sound of men and women's voices, low youthful laughs of people going home two by two. A phonograph was playing *Seconhand Rose*. [...] There came on the air through the window a sourness of garbage, a smell of burnt gasoline and traffic and dusty pavements, a huddled stuffiness of pigeonhole rooms where men and women's bodies writhed alone tortured by the night and the young summer (Passos 164).

The sensuous impressions are not only perceived as dissociated parts by the reader, but also by the characters of the novel itself. In a crowded subway, people are seen as "[e]lbows, packages, shoulders, buttocks" (125), not as individuals. This reveals another striking aspect of City life: impersonality and loneliness. This irony is observed and noticed by Jimmy Herf who is then finally able to leave New York behind.

By incorporating visual, acoustic and olfactory senses, Dos Passos wants to make his abstracted and fragmented scenes become more vivid, the pictures are set into motion and the City becomes what it is: "'[...] a city of cave-dwellers, with a frightful, brutal ugliness about it ...'" (Gates 78). In addition, this kind of technique imparts to New York a personality, so that one can rightfully say that Manhattan is the protagonist of *Manhattan Transfer*.

Dos Passos' treatment of time is another technique that contributes to the hectic and frantic atmosphere of the City. If one considers time as tempo, the life of the characters runs by as fast as the life of the City. "As odd moments in the lives of the characters receive stress and time intervals are chosen in an irregular pattern, the movement within the novel becomes syncopated" (Gelfant, "John Dos Passos: The Synoptic Novel" 148). But, if one considers time in the sense of years passing by and important moments, it is different for the City and its characters: "In Jimmy Herf's personal history, the moment when he marries Ellen may be crucial, but in the history of twentieth-century Manhattan this moment is inconsequential" (148). What is really important for New York is the change in social and economic tendencies, the transition of the celebrated metropolis to a world of disorder, crime and destruction. This is revealed by the old tramp at the end of the novel:

> Do you know how long God took to destroy the Tower of Babel, folks? Seven minutes. Do you know how long the Lord God took to destroy Babylon and Nineveh? Seven minutes. There's more wickedness in one block in New York City than there was in a square mile in Nineveh, and how long do you think the Lord God of Sabboath will take to destroy New York City and Brooklyn and the Bronx? Seven seconds. Seven seconds.... (Passos 323).

The structure of the novel, as already mentioned, ends where it has started years before. This means, there is a circular movement and seemingly no progress at all. This is pure irony, because in a crammed City where action is omnipresent in the most different ways, action is actually fruitless: "in the end, actions have cancelled each other, decisions have remained abortive and plans inchoate, and time has defeated one's hopes in the city" (Gelfant, "John Dos Passos: The Synoptic Novel" 149). This is also evident in some of the characters of *Manhattan Transfer*. Congo Jake, a former French sailor has become the millionaire Armand Duval, but in fact he has to face jail, because of his profession as bootlegger in the times of Prohibition (1920s). He may be rich, but that did not get him anywhere but behind bars. All his efforts were ceaseless.

Furthermore, Dos Passos uses urban symbolism that "functions both to create the city as a place and atmosphere and to define its underlying social implications as a way of life" (152). The chapter headings, the epigraphs and a lot of textual references such as biblical references, excerpts from magazines or newspapers, jingles or phrases serve as symbols and can be interpreted as implicit criticism of twentieth-century Manhattan. When reading the chapter *Went to the Animals' Fair*, it becomes clear that the City itself is a giant Animals' Fair, where people "go round and round in a squirrel cage" (Passos 187). Despite the hugeness of New York the people feel imprisoned because, as George Baldwin says, "[t]he terrible thing about having New York go stale on you is that there's nowhere else. It's the top of the world" (187). The chapters *Steamroller, Fire Engine, One More River to Jordan and the Burthen of Nineveh* reveal the destructiveness of New York, whereas *Skyscrapers* can be interpreted in two ways. It stands on the one hand for the beauty, but on the other hand also for the power of the metropolis. The architects Specker and Sandbourne dream of a magnificent City made of steel and glass (cf. Passos 63), but being drunk, Jimmy sees a skyscraper falling on him with the picture of Ellen in its windows. To him the City poses a threat, a destructive power, so that he decides to leave New York behind and start all over. Moreover, *Revolving Doors* can be interpreted in terms of the monotony and routine of business life "in which the time clock establishes man's pace, while revolving doors feed him 'in a tape and out [...] noon and night and morning, [...] grinding out [...] years like sausage meat'" (Gelfant, "John Dos Passos: The Synoptic Novel" 155).

Also the characters in *Manhattan Transfer* are presented in a very abstract way, they are just flash shots in the already dissociate scenes of the novel. This gives the author the chance to focus entirely on the City itself, because the lives of the individuals are subordinated to the patterns of New York City. The characters lack a proper identity due to the fact that the City fosters dissociation and dehumanization. This is also revealed in the way the characters' development is portrayed. Seemingly unrelated and unimportant incidents in their lives are emphasized and described but with no overt connection whatsoever. As Blanche Gelfant has pointed out, Ellen is one example for this phenomenon, because she "appears in disjointed images that show her at various moments in her life, but these images do not imply casual relationships nor show how or why one image comes to supersede another" (160). The people living in the City become marionettes in the hand of the puppeteer Manhattan. This impressionistic technique is also part of Dos Passos' intention to criticize the moral temper of twentieth-century New York, because the characters

> represent, like the chaotic setting, the din, stench, and cacophony of the city, the nerve-racking pace, the jagged tempo, the symbols of doom, and the structure of futility,

14

an undercurrent of social tensions that Dos Passos interpreted to be creating the most tragic moment in American
history (166).

Taking all analyzed elements into account, one can argue that New York City
in *Manhattan Transfer* represents the tragic transition from virtue to vice.
The technique of abstraction together with the constant assault of the human
senses establishes the City as the main protagonist and functions as a means
of social as well as economic commentary. The treatment of time and the
urban symbols show the real character of New York, that action is ceaseless
and that New York exerts a unbearable power on its inhabitants with almost
no way out. What follows is the cult of the self: They all lose their identity
and become aggressive and selfish human beings. Appearance becomes more
important than substance, they have to realize that their dreams will never
become true, and moral values are considered unimportant.

As a consequence, the City is a metaphor for a modern Babylon, for
which reason the author has fittingly chosen to put the following epigraph
under the chapter *Metropolis*:

> There were Babylon and Nineveh; they were built of brick.
> Athens was gold marble columns. Rome was held up on
> broad arches of rubble. In Constantinople the minarets
> flame like great candles round the Golden Horn... Steel,
> glass, tile, concrete will be the materials of the skyscrap-
> ers. Crammed on the narrow island the millionwindowed
> buildings will just glittering, pyramid on pyramid like the
> white cloudhead above a thunderstorm (Passos 11).

3.2 Into the City

3.2.1 The Polarized City of Edith Wharton's *The House of Mirth* and Stephen Crane's *Maggie: A Girl of the Streets*

Stephen Crane (1871-1900) published his first novel *Maggie: A Girl of the
Streets* in March 1893 at his own expenses under the pseudonym "Johnston
Smith". Since he was a young author who still had to establish himself in
the world of writing, he "was cautious about immediately identifying himself
with a work that he himself regarded as shocking" (Crane x). The reason is

his heroine Maggie, who is drawn into prostitution and finally dies due to the brutal environment of New York City. Stephen Crane immersed himself in the New York Bowery, the main setting of the novella, and the experiences he gained in the East Side slums created this work.

Edith Wharton (1862-1937) was born into a wealthy family of the Old New York Society. She published *The House of Mirth* in 1905, which brought her international fame as a writer. Wharton knew "high society - its glittering extremes and its pitfalls" (Gates 30) and so she tells the story of Lily Bart, "glamorous, single, hanging on by her slender pink fingernails to New York high society, and desperate for a rich husband to secure her place in the Manhattan social elite" (Beer xii).

In their novels both authors focus on the part of the City they know best - Stephen Crane on the poor working-class people living in the Bowery district and Edith Wharton on the rich, who reside in mansions on the Upper East Side. This polarized City came into existence due to the mechanisms of industrialization, urbanization and a growing sense for materialism. Therefore, the gap between rich and poor widened and was responsible for the development of the East Side slums as "a district that in Crane's day was becoming synonymous with poverty and the attendant vices of filth, drink, crime, and degradation" (Crane xvii). What is quite interesting is the fact that despite the opposite focus of each of the novels, they conclude surprisingly similar.

> New York as a socially polarized city is an unhealthy city for, as in Edith Wharton's novel, the inhabitants live out their lives in insulated, greedy splendor, or as in Stephen Crane, they end up as drunkards and prostitutes (Gates 30).

The question that needs to be analyzed here is: What makes the City unhealthy? In a letter to Hamlin Garland, Crane pointed out that "environment is a tremendous thing in the world and frequently shapes lives regardless" (Sorrentino 82). Taking a closer look at the word 'environment' itself one can observe that the term is ambiguous. On the surface the term only seems to describe the external living conditions of the people, but both Edith Wharton and Stephen Crane also referred to the mental influences, such as certain expectations or institutions like the Church and the theater, that constantly affect society. Thus, the lives of Lily Bart and Maggie Johnson are unhealthy, because their living conditions and mental influences determine their path of life.

In theory, the novels *Maggie: A Girl of the Streets* and *The House of Mirth* are very realistic for they try to be as accurate and detailed as possible in their descriptions of the settings. But in practice, they go beyond realism. Their message is clearly naturalistic[9] when stating that people were determined by their environment and heredity. The social reformer Herbert Spencer applied Darwin's theory of the "survival of the fittest" to society and pointed out that only the fittest would survive the change of New York to an industrial nation. This fostered an elbow society in which old morals and values collapsed and possessions became more and more important.

That *Maggie* is one of the major works to criticize the environment of late 19th century New York City becomes obvious when the reader notices that the protagonist Maggie does neither occur in the first, nor in the last chapter of the novella. Furthermore, the very title of the 1893 version *Maggie: A Girl of the Streets (A Story of New York)* indicates that the author is at least as concerned with the City as with Maggie.

The place, the novella is set in, derives its name from the Dutch word *bowerij* and means "farm". It was a farming area north of the City and at the time about 1800 a very fashionable place. After the Civil War, the Bowery had to compete with Broadway and Fifth Avenue and step by step this area became the place as the reader can encounter it in Crane's story:

> [A] dark region where, from a careening building, a dozen gruesome doorways gave up loads of babies to the street and gutter. [...] Long streamers of garments fluttered from

---

[9] "Naturalism is a form of realism which also involves the accumulation and documentation of minute details but which distinguishes itself from realism through its application of the principles of biology and social science, pioneered by Darwin and Spencer, to the depiction of individuals. [...], [N]aturalistic texts typically present characters, often in an urban setting, who are incapable of exercising free will, whose lives, like those of insects or animals, are directed by external forces and whose fates are determined by heredity, environment and economics" (Beer 77).

fire escapes. In all unhandy places there were buckets, brooms, rags and bottles. In the street infants played or fought with other infants or sat stupidly in the way of vehicles. [...] A thousand odors of cooking food came forth to the street. The building quivered and creaked from the weight of humanity stamping about it in its bowels (Crane 7).

These first few lines give a short glance at how people used to live at the end of the 19th century. It is a dark place with children playing in the dirt. It does not smell very pleasant and the reader can virtually hear the creaking and noisiness of the place. Within the whole novel, times and again Crane gives descriptions of the outside world of the Bowery. He does so, because the life of his characters is mostly situated out on the streets and only partly inside their houses. This can be seen from the fact that the novel starts out on "Devil's Row" (3) and also ends outside the tenements at the East River.

The Bowery is described like a battlefield where everyone fights against each other: Be it Jimmie who battles "Devil's Row"(3) or Maggie's constantly drunken mother Mary who throws herself upon Maggie for breaking a plate (cf. Crane 11). This violence is fostered by a huge abuse of alcohol. People start drinking because they "seek release from their destiny" (Stallman 74), which is a life in poverty with no way out. Therefore, Pizer argues that the place is like a prison (cf. Pizer 188). Even children get confronted with alcoholism at a very early age. They either have to buy it for their parents or neighbors like Jimmie, who "[takes] a tendered tin-pail and seven pennies and depart[s]. He passe[s] into the side door of a saloon and [goes] to the bar" (Crane 13), or they start drinking themselves. Alcoholism leads then directly back to the problem of violence, which turns life in the Bowery into a vicious circle.

A term that describes the people in the Bowery best is 'variety'. Jacob Riis[10] writes that "[a] map of the city, colored to designate nationalities, would show more stripes than on the skin of a zebra, and more colors than

---

[10]Jacob A. Riis was a social reformer, photographer, and writer. He emigrated from Denmark to the United States in 1870. After he witnessed the great poverty and overcrowded houses in the Bowery, he became an advocate for immigrants and wrote the bestseller *How the Other Half Lives* with many photographs to illustrate the circumstances. He helped improving the living conditions in the tenements of New York.

any window" (Riis 75). He goes on: "One may find [...] an Italian, a German, a French, African, Spanish, Bohemian, Russian, Scandinavian, Jewish, and Chinese colony" (73).

The tenements were "multiple-unit residential buildings" (Jackson, *The Encyclopedia of New York City* 1161) and provided compact rental housing for poor and working-class immigrants living and working in lower Manhattan. They all had a very typical appearance, were made of brick and four to six stories high. There was always a dark staircase in the center of the building and almost no light and ventilation due to the lack of windows and airshafts. Jacob Riis writes that "if we could see the air breathed by these poor creatures [...], it would show itself to be fouler than the mud of the gutters" (Riis 65). The houses were crammed with more than a hundred residents, though a five-story tenement was designed for only 20 families. Additionally, only a third of the people had running water and consequently the danger for epidemics and death was quite high.

Stephen Crane uses similar adjectives describing the tenement of the Johnson family. There are "dark stairways", "cold, gloomy halls", "dark, dust-stained walls" and "scant and crude furniture" (Crane 8-9) that altogether form their home. Because of this environment, the baby Tommie and also the father of Maggie die early in the novella. Furthermore, Maggie dies at the end of the novella being a victim of her environment, whereas Jimmie inevitably becomes the replica of his father.

Let alone from the description of the Bowery and the tenements, it becomes clear that New York City is a place conspicuous for alcoholism, homelessness, poverty, prostitution and crime. It is no wonder that Maggie tries to escape from this environment by indulging herself "in illusions of happiness and grandeur derived from the theater, the saloon, [...] and the mission house" (Stallman 74). In the novella, Maggie visits a Vaudeville theater together with her lover Pete. They watch a typical late-19th century melodrama with a "brain-clutching heroine" who wants to be rescued by the "hero with the beautiful sentiments" and the "villains", who tyrannize "aged strangers" (Crane 37). The spectators are convinced that this is "transcendental realism"

(37) and that the actors and actresses on stage not only play their characters, but also embody them. This can be seen when "[w]ith untiring zeal they [the visitors] hiss[...] vice and applaud[...] virtue" or when they "encourage[...] the the struggling hero with cries, and jeer[...] the villain, hooting and calling attention to his whiskers" (38). After the hero finally manages to defeat the villain, Maggie departs "with raised spirits [...]. She rejoice[s] the way in which the poor and virtuous eventually surmount[...] the wealthy and wicked" (38).

Evidently, for Maggie the theater portrays the ideals of rising above the Rum Alley environment and escaping from the tenements and Bowery life. Maggie naively accepts the melodrama as real life and "wonder[s] if the culture and refinement she had seen imitated, [...], by the heroine on the stage, [can] be acquired by a girl who live[s] in a tenement house and work[s] in a shirt factory" (38). Only in the end, when she is rejected by Pete and her family, she realizes that her dream will never become reality. The reason is provided by the naturalistic assumption that outer forces determine her life. Here, this force is the theater that gives Maggie false and romantic illusions and therefore contributes to her downfall.

The Church is another institution that helps Stephen Crane to establish New York as an unhealthy environment. It used to be a special place of worship, prayer and the confession of sins, but with *Maggie* Crane wants to reveal that there is a change in moral values and that the Church

> has become, [...], subsidized by gold, saying in effect 'I am rich and increased in goods and have no need of nothing;' apparently ignorant of the fact that she [...] has failed in her true mission - that of establishing on earth an ideal brotherhood (Flower 89).

After Maggie has been sent "[...] teh hell" by her family and Pete, she wanders alone through "rottling avenues and passe[s] between rows of houses" until she encounters "a stout gentleman in a silk hat and a chaste black coat, [...]" (Crane 74). When she recognizes the man to be a clergyman, she decides to approach him for she "had heard of the Grace of God" (74). Maggie is convinced of the benevolence, kindheartedness and goodwill of the minister. Unfortunately, it turns out to be only a façade, because she is fooled again when the minister "gave a convulsive movement and saved his respectability by a vigorous side-step. He did not risk to save a soul. For how was he to know that there was a soul before him that needed saving?" (74). He simply steps aside and signals Maggie that he does not want to help her. For him "respectability"(74) is more important than a girl's soul, which shows the minister's ignorance of his own principles. Crane shows effectively how the circumstances have changed and that the Church has ended up on a path of indifference, coldheartedness and self-interest. The preset ideal of being a refuge and a helping hand in all living conditions makes Maggie believe that she could be saved, but in fact it makes her commit suicide.

The two mental determinants influence not only Maggie but also her family, who draw their morality almost entirely "from a middle-class ethic which stresses the home as the center of virtue, and respectability as the primary moral goal" (Pizer 185). They incorrectly apply them to themselves and with that jostle Maggie off the edge. She gets abandoned by her brother Jimmie, who shortly reflects on whether or not to forsake his sister in favor of his position in society:

> Of course Jimmie publicly damned his sister that he might appear on a higher social plane. But, arguing with himself, stumbling about in ways that he knew not, he once, almost came to a conclusion that his sister would have been more firmly good had she better known why. However, he felt that he could not hold such a view. He threw it hastily aside (Crane 60).

In the end, he does not forgive her, as well as her mother Mary, who casts her out as a bad seed and sends her to the devil in front of the whole tenement neighborhood, because she is "a disgrace teh [her] people" (42). She is not allowed to live at home anymore since she has lost her virtuousness and soul by having been seduced by Pete. Crane pushes his reader to see the hypocrisy of the moral codes, which condemn sexual conduct more fully than they condemn cruelty and rejection. Especially in a City like New York, this hypocrisy becomes prevalent since there is no buffer between the two polarized classes, in a topographical and social sense. New York is divided by an invisible line into two parts: Rich people dwell in Uptown and Midtown regions, whereas the Downtown area is the home of the underprivileged.

Maggie is left alone, isolated from her family, rejected by her former lover Pete and the clergyman. Robert A. Gates stresses that all the characters in the novel are surrounded by a general sense of isolation (cf. Gates 54). This is a paradox since City life actually precludes physical isolation, but Stephen Crane portrays this indifference of nature brilliantly in chapter one of the novella:

> From a window of an apartment house that upreared its form from amid squat, ignorant stables, there leaned a curious woman. Some laborers, unloading a scow at a dock at the river, paused for a moment and regarded the fight. The engineer of a passive tugboat hung lazily to a railing and watched. Over on the Island, a worm of yellow convicts came from the shadow of a grey ominous building and crawled slowly along the river's bank (4).

The woman, the engineer, the laborers and the convicts are all part of the action, but at the same time also separated from it. New York creates due to its crammed streets and houses the illusion of being a community, but in fact each character is left to its own.

This isolation, generated through the morally illiterate people living in the Bowery and the deterministic forces of the Church and the theater, forces Maggie out on the streets. Nevertheless, it is a place she is quite familiar with since the life of the Bowery dwellers mostly takes place outside their homes. She becomes a nameless, "girl of the painted cohorts of the city" (76). Maggie is quite a successful prostitute in Midtown, since she goes along "glittering avenues" wearing a "handsome cloak" (76), but after a time she has to move to places further in the south of New York, assumably because men lost their interest in her. She passes a "concert hall", arrives "in the gloomy districts near the river" and goes "into the blackness of the final block" (77). "At [the girls'] feet the river appeared a deathly black hue" and finally "[t]he varied sounds of life, [...], came faintly and died away to a silence" (78). Also the various men she encounters represent this downfall, for they are at the beginning quite handsome and at the end only "ragged being[s] with shifting, blood shot eyes and grimey hands" (77). Maggie dies committing suicide in the East River and thus, her life ends where she started it: At home, the Bowery of

New York City.

New York City and its unhealthy environment prove to be fatal for Maggie. She is trapped within her class, isolated from everybody she held dear and finally only a nameless victim in the metropolis for she lacked the ability to adapt to the cruel and hypocritical world of the Bowery, unlike her mother Mary, her brother Jimmie and Pete. Her death was inevitable since she was not as fit as the other characters and therefore was determined to die. That is why Manhattan can be interpreted as a metaphor for a deterministic life in a tremendous environment.

With *The House of Mirth* Edith Wharton reveals the other side of New York, at least in terms of the social hierarchy. Lily Bart, her friends and acquaintances all live above 49th Street in mansions that "were truly grandiose and represented practically every architectural style imaginable as each merchant attempted to excel his neighbor in magnificence and splendor" (Gates 30). The well-off habitants of New York City wanted to show off their fortune and so

> the Vanderbilt mansion competed for attention with the cream-colored Touraine Chateau at the northeast corner of 56th Street built by William Waldorf Astor. Nearby the ominous grey stone palazzo of Collis P. Huntington, the California railroad magnet, loomed majestically on 57th Street (30).

Since Edith Wharton's characters mostly live inside their grand houses, one has to look keenly for descriptions of the streets and public places Lily dwells on. Often street names, such as Fifth Avenue or Madison Avenue are mentioned, but then there is no further description given (cf. Wharton 7). When Lily stands in front of Seldon's house, a close friend of hers, the reader gets a small impression of New York's upper-class: "She glanced with interest along the new brick and limestone house-fronts, fantastically varied in obedience to the American craving for novelty [..] She looked across at the flat-house with its marble porch and pseudo-Georgian façade"(Wharton 8). Beside these rare passages, New York and its streets are described in a very negative way, they pose a threat to Lily. This becomes clear when she arrives at Grand Central Station in early September and complains about the stuffy atmosphere she is welcomed with: "Oh dear, I'm so hot and thirsty - and what a hideous place New York is! [...] Other cities put on their best clothes in summer, but New York seems to sit in its shirt-sleeves" (7). Manhattan weighs down upon Lily, no matter what season, because also "[t]he New York winter had presented an interminable perspective of snow-burdened days, reaching toward a spring of raw sunshine and furious air, when the ugliness of things rasped the eye as the gritty wind ground into the skin" (179). Only one time the City becomes a cheerful and pleasant place. This is after Lily died from an overdose of sedatives:

> The next morning rose mild and bright, with a promise of summer in the air. The sunlight slanted joyously down Lily's street, mellowed the blistered house-front, gilded the paintless railings of the door-step, and struck prismatic glories from the panes of her darkened window (315).

It seems as if the City is a personified demon that finally succeeded in defeating Lily. Now after her death, Manhattan puts on its mask of joy and splendor, but as soon as it has found its next innocent victim, New York again will show its real and cruel face.

That interiors take a very important position in the lives of the characters shows the title of the novel. It is called *The House of Mirth*, so one can assume that most of the action takes place inside the house. It seems to be a kind of refuge from the cruel streets. Again and again, Edith Wharton gives descriptions of the interior of the houses in order to indicate that appearance and a special sense of taste is an important issue in the world of the rich. In the third chapter Lily describes the Bellomont mansion from the inside:

> The hall was arcaded, with a gallery supported on columns of pale yellow marble. Tall clumps of flowering plants were grouped against a background of dark foliage in the angles of the walls. On the crimson carpet a deer-hound and two or three spaniels dozed luxuriously before the fire, and the light from the great central lantern overhead shed a brightness on the women's hair and struck sparks from their jewels as they moved (26).

The place is decorated with luxurious objects, such as marble, valuable plants, carpets and a fire place. At those times dogs were only affordable when money was not an issue, and all the women wore precious jewels to show off their wealthy lifestyle. It represents the ideal home for Lily, a cozy place where one can feel comfortable and where one has the feeling of belonging. For Lily, feeling at home is part of constructing an identity for herself, which is the reason for her to say that if she "could only do over [her] aunt's drawing-room", she would be "a better woman" (9).

It is Lily Bart's environment that prevents her from achieving a complete self. This is already foreshadowed at the beginning of the novel. Lily just missed her train at Grand Central Station, which can be interpreted as a metaphor for her life, which is predetermined by society. Mr. Seldon aptly summarizes her situation as follows: "She was so evidently the victim of the civilization which had produced her, that the links of her bracelet seemed like manacles chaining her to her fate" (9). Lily has no free will, she is literally chained to her fate, and there is no way out. Edith Wharton blames money and an ever increasing will for power to be responsible for the decay of moral values and ideals and therefore also for Lily's fall. "Surrounded by the rich and powerful, Lily soon learns that money brings with it an almost invincible power, but a power that crushes and subverts the finer instincts in man" (Gates 38). Simon Rosedale serves as a good example to show that money rules life in New York City. He is an outcast of society because he is a Jew, but within the course of the novel he becomes one of the most powerful acquaintances of Lily. He bought himself into the ranks of the New York high-society, because money is "the principal determiner of acceptance within the City" (38). Another character that proves economic determinism is Bertha Dorset. She falsely accuses Lily of adultery in order to conceal her own extramarital affairs and succeeds in the end due to her higher social position. She is richer than Lily and therefore it does not occur to the people to question this accusation. They simply believe the words of Mrs. Dorset.

According to Blanche Housman Gelfant, "[h]ypocrisy, indifference, pettiness, narrow convention, and insensibility - [...] are not merely the flaws within a society: they *are* fashionable New York" (Gelfant, "The Destructive Element" 115). All these factors lead to an overall feeling of rootlessness for

Lily, which she expresses toward the end of the novel:

> That was the feeling which possessed her now, the feeling
> of being something rootless and ephemeral, mere spindrift
> of the whirling surface of existence, without anything to
> which the poor little tentacles of self could cling before the
> awful flood submerged them. And as she looked back she
> saw that there had never been a time when she had any real
> relation to life. Her parents too had been rootless, blown
> hither and thither on every wind of fashion, without any
> personal existence to shelter them from its shifting gusts.
> She herself had grown up without any one spot of earth
> being dearer to her than another; there was no centre of
> early pieties, of grave endearing traditions, to which her
> heart could revert and from which it could draw strength
> for itself and tenderness for others (Wharton 310).

Lily realizes that she never had a place she could call home, where she could feel comfortable. Until the end, she moves from place to place and what should feel like home to Lily, namely her room at her aunt's house Mrs. Peniston, does not fulfill its function: "To a torn heart uncomforted by human nearness a room may open almost human arms, and the being to whom no four walls mean more than any others, is, at such hours, expatriate everywhere" (146).

Moreover, Lily mentions the lack of tradition that could have given her the strength to survive in this unhealthy environment of New York. The well-off upper class is not interested in traditions, they are more concerned about surfaces, how their houses look like from the outside as well as from the inside, how people are dressed and what kind of amusements they visit in order to be seen. This is effectively expressed in the title of the novel. Wharton quite clearly alludes to a quote from the King James Bible:

> It is better to go to the house of mourning, than to go to
> the house of feasting: for that is the end of all men; and
> the living will lay it to his heart.
> Sorrow is better than laughter: for by the sadness of the
> countenance the heart is made better.
> The heart of the wise is in the house of mourning; but the
> heart of fools is in the house of mirth ("The King James
> Bible" Ecclesiastes 7:2-4).

It is Edith Wharton herself who is the "wise" and her heart is in "the house of mourning" for she really mourns the moral failures of the ruthless upper class of Manhattan. They do not "have second thoughts or the slightest misgivings about sacrificing one of their own - in this case Lily - in order to cover up their own shortcomings and moral depravity" (Sauter 139). Consequently, the "fools" are Lily's acquaintances who dwell in "the house of mirth", "running endlessly after entertainment and merriment" (139).

Due to the fact that Lily is an outcast of society, she becomes isolated, which is an "intrinsic problem of a large, impersonal city such as New York" (Gates 41) according to Edith Wharton. This isolation can be seen from three different angles. First, she becomes economically isolated from her friends because she is not able to live among them as equal anymore. At the Trenor's house, she starts playing bridge although she knows she cannot afford it and has to recognize:

> A few years ago it had sufficed her: she had taken her daily
> meed of pleasure without caring who provided it. Now she
> was beginning to chafe at the obligations it imposed, to
> feel herself a mere pensioner on the splendour which had
> once seemed to belong to her (Wharton 27).

Lily becomes socially isolated after her aunt disinherited her. Here, Lily feels utterly alone for the first time: "No one looked at her, no one seemed aware of her presence; she was probing the very depth of insignificance" (217). She becomes a total outcast when Lily is accused of adultery by Bertha Dorset. She backs out and rejects every offer of moral or financial support by Gerty Farish or Simon Rosedale.

Her spiritual isolation is fostered by a narcotic drug, which will finally kill her at the end of the novel. One evening at Bryant Park, Lily has lost her power to fight for a comfortable, financially secure life in the upper class of New York:

> That melancholy pleasure-ground was almost deserted when
> she entered it, and she sank down on an empty bench in the
> glare of an electric street lamp. The warmth of the fire had
> passed out of her veins, and she told herself that she must
> not sit long in the penetrating dampness which struck up
> from the wet asphalt. But her will-power seemed to have
> spent itself in a last great effort, and she was lost in the
> blank reaction which follows on an unwonted expenditure
> of energy (302).

Lily's isolation mirrors the deterministic forces of the City. Every individual is on his own and everyone has to look after himself[11]. Taking the problems of rootlessness and isolation together, one can say that they dehumanize the characters of *The House of Mirth*. People are forced into behavior patterns and can not escape from them without consequences - fatal consequences in the case of Lily.

The downward spiral towards Lily's sad end is represented in the housing situation as home and comfort are very important factors in her life. Everything is set in motion when Lily stands "[o]n the doorstep, with the street before her" (145) after visiting the Trenor's mansion. Lily has to realize that her status as a marriageable girl has changed to a single woman with a very dubious reputation and quite tellingly "she note[s] the mute aspect of Fifth Avenue" (145). With that also Lily's self image is affected negatively, because "[s]he seem[s] a stranger to herself. [...] She open[s] her eyes and [sees] the streets passing - the familiar alien streets. All she look[s] on [is] the same and yet changed [...]" (145). New York makes Lily feel "alone in a place of darkness and pollution" (145) so that she has the impression that, after her aunt Mrs. Peniston passed away, the "future stretche[s] before her dull and bare as the deserted Fifth Avenue" (225). This prominent street also changes its significance for Lily since she once needed "an atmosphere of luxury; [...] it was the only climate she could breathe in" (2), but now Fifth Avenue becomes a hideous place, full of dirt with no option to breathe freely. Lily's last station in her downward movement is "to give up her apartment, and shrink to the obscurity of a boarding-house" (260) far away from her former neighborhood. It is not luxurious at all, decorated with "blotched wall-paper and shabby paint" and the streets make her whole life feel like a "degradation [...] in the last stages of decline [...]" (280). She is rootless and isolated from her former life in a physical and spiritual sense and so only the drug manages to make Lily feel joyous in her last thoughts before she dies: "She ha[s] been unhappy, and now she [is] happy - she ha[s] felt herself alone, and now the sense of loneliness ha[s] vanished"(314) and then "warmth flow[s] through her once more, she yield[s]

---

[11]This is what Dos Passos has called the cult of the self.

to it, [sinks] into it, and [sleeps]"(315).

Lily Bart has to die as a victim of her New York society, because she is not adapted to the circumstances in the fast-changing environment of the metropolis that Lily herself calls a "great civic machine" (268). She is not able to open the doors of her "gilt cage"(55) and thus, is doomed to die. This is the reason why New York can be classified as a giant deterministic cage in which the "fools"("The King James Bible") dwell and from which Lily only could free herself after committing suicide.

3.3 The Metaphysical City

3.3.1 Paul Auster's *City of Glass*

The citation "[i]t made no sense, and because of that, it made all the sense in the world" (Auster 294) written by Paul Auster (*1947) himself mirrors the very character of the metaphysical detective story that deals with Daniel Quinn, also a writer of detective fiction, who tries to understand the postmodern City of New York, but fails miserably. He is not able to find a solution to his case and thus, everything remains uncertain and unreliable until the very end.

City of Glass (1985) is the first part of three books that together form *The New York Trilogy* and was first published as a single volume in 1988. It is a postmodern piece of writing and carries therefore certain typical characteristics that have influenced Quinn on his way through the maze of New York in search for the ultimate truth.

> Postmodernism is largely a reaction to the assumed certainty of scientific, or objective, efforts to explain reality. In essence, it stems from a recognition that reality is not simply mirrored in human understanding of it, but rather, is constructed as the mind tries to understand its own particular and personal reality. [...] In the postmodern understanding, interpretation is everything; reality only comes into being through our interpretations of what the world means to us individually. Postmodernism relies on concrete experience over abstract principles, knowing always that the outcome of one's own experience will necessarily be fallible and relative, rather than certain and universal (Kick 13).

What is of considerable importance for the novel, is the construction of reality, as will become clear in a later step. The relationship between fiction and reality is questioned in postmodern writing and can be summarized in the term 'metafiction'. This particular character becomes apparent in the first chapter, when Daniel Quinn reveals to the reader that he had "long ago stopped thinking of himself as real" (Auster 9). Closely related to this element is the importance of language. According to the principle of logocentrism, language is able to describe reality in an exact way, which is deeply questioned and replaced by a general sense of skepticism. Daniel Quinn himself has made language his profession since he is a writer of detective fiction and later gets involved into an investigation about the origin of language. He employs the traditional conventions of the detective story whose roots can be located in the writings of Edgar Allen Poe. He coined the characteristics of these stories with his work *Tales of Mystery and Imagination*: "Die Handlung des Detektivromans beschäftigt sich in erster Linie mit der psychologischen Situation des Täters oder dem eigentlichen Tathergang; von Interesse ist lediglich die Aufklärung des Verbrechens" (Hoffarth 4). What Quinn likes about these traditional conventions, is that the detective is always able to restore law and order in his world, for "[t]he detective is the one who looks, who listens, who moves through this morass of objects and events in search of the thought, the idea that will pull all these things together and make sense of them"(Auster 8). There will always be a solution to the cases of Max Work, the protagonist of Daniel Quinn's stories. It becomes clear that language, at least for Quinn, is able to depict reality, because

> [i]n the good mystery there is nothing wasted, no sentence, no word that is not significant. And even if it is not significant, it has the potential to be so - which amounts to the same thing. The world of the books comes to life, seething with possibilities, with secrets and contradictions. Since everything seen or said, even the slightest, most trivial thing, can bear a connection to the outcome of the story, nothing must be overlooked (8).

Paul Auster is more conspicuous about language and its relation to reality for he constructs the New York Quinn lives in by making use of the so-called 'metaphysical detective novel'. He turns his back on the conventional English archetype of the detective novel and thus, achieves a literary approach to urban reality of modern America. Mr. Hoffarth explains the development from the conventional form to the new one as follows

> Der maßgebliche Unterschied zwischen der 'Anti-Detective-Novel' und den vorhergehenden Formen besteht insbesondere in ihrer parodistischen Ausgestaltung des Schlusses - die Aufklärung des Falles, die Verkündigung der Lösung als zentrales Element der Handlung bleibt dem Leser verborgen" (Hoffarth 7).

Finally, everything will end up in confusion, isolation and meaninglessness, because the detective himself is not able to decode the collection of signs properly that were provided by the postmodern City.

It is Mr. Stillman Senior, the man Quinn has to observe after taking up the case of Mrs. Stillman and Mr. Stillman Junior, who first seems to realize that language has lost its original meaning for he wants to know if God had a language and if it was possible to restore it. Therefore he used his son Peter and isolated him at the age of two for nine years from his familiar surroundings and stopped talking to him in his presence. Daniel Quinn, now carrying the identity of the detective Paul Auster, meets Stillman Jr. for the first time a few days before his father is to be released from prison. What seems striking to Quinn is the fact that "[e]verything about Peter Stillman [is] white" (Auster 15) which can be interpreted as a metaphoric reflection of his personal as well as linguistic blankness. His movements and language are dominated by instability, amorphousness and arbitrariness so that Quinn fittingly compares him to a marionette "trying to walk without strings" (15). When Peter starts to tell his story, he utters phrases and word chunks that neither the reader nor Quinn is able to read. These words do not seem to be expressed willfully and some even appear to be made up, such as "mumbo jumbo", "[w]illy nilly" and "[n]incompoop" (16). Obviously, Peter is not the master of his own utterances, but language masters him instead. The reason for Peter Stillman to voice all the words and phrases is given after he has told Quinn his story: "I say what they say because I know nothing" (16), which supports Quinn's impression of Peter being a marionette.

To put it in other words, language does not express what we really mean.

Consequently, Quinn's task, as a detective, to read and correctly interpret the meaning of Stillman Sr.'s doings on the street and its connection to the case must inevitably end up in a one-way street. In linguistic terms, there happens to be a lack of congruence between the signifier, which refers to the word, and the signified, being the denoted item (cf. Herzogenrath 25). Stillman explains this incongruence to Quinn by using the example of an umbrella:

> Not only is an umbrella a thing, it is a thing that performs a function - in other words, expresses the will of man. [...] What happens when a thing no longer performs its function? [...] Because it can no longer perform its function, the umbrella has ceased to be an umbrella. It might resemble an umbrella, it might once have been an umbrella, but now it has changed into something else. The word, however, has remained the same. Therefore, it can no longer express the thing (Auster 77).

Quinn is not able to match words and things as well, but he does not recognize his situation consciously. This can be seen on several occasions in the book. In chapter seven, he is not able to "grasp the connection between the constellations and their names" (51) when studying the fresco of constellations on the ceiling of Grand Central Station. Moreover, a few pages later, Quinn is confronted with the problem of identifying the real Peter Stillman Sr. since the two men both resemble the man on the picture that Quinn got from Mrs. Stillman. Finally he notices: "Whatever choice he made - [...] - would be arbitrary, a submission to chance" (56).

Postmodern America, and especially New York, therefore needs a new language, one "that at last say what we have to say", because the words "have not adapted themselves to the new reality"(77). The result is chaos and a constant danger for misunderstandings. According to Stillman Sr., this situation is noticeable especially in New York City, "the most forlorn of places, the most abject. The brokenness is everywhere, the disarray is universal. [...] The broken people, the broken things, the broken thoughts. The whole city is a junk heap" (78). Mrs. Dallmann argues, that Stillman tries to establish a parallel between the broken character of language and the fragmentation of the individual in the metropolis (cf. Dallmann 359).

The reason for such a development in New York City is established on the very first page of the novel *City of Glass*: "Nothing is real except of chance" (3), which means that there is a constant change in the City. Signifier and signified will never match because, as Paul Auster puts it, "[o]ur lives don't really belong to us, [...] - they belong to the world, and in spite of our efforts to make sense of it, the world is a place beyond our understanding" [12]. Quinn does not see that the City is just too complex to be understood and thus, loses himself in a fruitless search through the chaotic streets of Manhattan. He even buys a red notebook, because he thinks that "[i]t would be helpful to have a separate place to record his thoughts, his observations, and his questions. In that way, perhaps, things might no get out of control" (38). But trying to make a readable text from the fragmented parts he records, does not help him to clear his sight at all. In fact, the City proves to be unreadable to Quinn from the very beginning: "New York was an inexhaustible space, a labyrinth of endless steps, and no matter how far he walked, no matter how well he came to know its neighborhoods and streets, it always left him with the feeling of being lost" (3f.).

Another element that is closely connected to writing in the red notebook is the act of walking in the City. At first, walking is a means of leaving the real world behind. During that time, Quinn is "[l]ost, not only in the city, but within himself as well. Each time he [takes] a walk, he [feels] as though he [is] leaving himself behind, and by giving himself up to the movement of the streets, by reducing himself to a seeing eye, he [is] able to escape the obligation to think, [...]"(4). Reality is dull and meaningless for Quinn, for he has lost his wife and child some years ago and has no friends. This explains his affinity with detective fiction, since his detective Max Work allows Quinn "to vanish, to withdraw into the confines of a strange and hermetic life, [...]"(9). Taking over the identity of Paul Auster, Quinn eventually begins his work on the Stillman case and "his walks cease to be about losing himself and are transformed into efforts to place the other inside a definitely bounded or mapped space" (Swope 9). On his walks through the streets of New York, Quinn records every

---

[12]This quote is taken from an interview with Paul Auster and Larry McCaffery and Sinda Gregory, *The Red Notebook*. Boston: Faber & Faber, 1995.

detail of Stillman Sr.'s movements in his red notebook. The City, thus, turns into a text which establishes the link between language and walking. A text consists of different written words and writing itself is the language of symbols. Stillman collects seemingly invaluable objects from the street, "[s]tones, leaves, and twigs all found their way into his bag"(Auster 60). Quinn does not understand Stillman's efforts, is not able to connect them in any way to the case itself and soon has to ask himself "if he had not embarked on a meaningless project" (60).

As a detective, it becomes Quinn's deepest desire to decode what he sees, "no matter how obscure"(69) and therefore he begins to translate his notes into little maps (cf. Auster 66-69). Quinn actually finds meaning in the letters that Stillman seems to 'write' on the surface of the City every day. After eleven days, Quinn thinks to read that he "has has been leaving a text of footsteps that spell out 'THE TOWER OF BABEL[13]', a topic, [...], on which Stillman published a book prior to his incarceration"(Swope 9). Matter of factly, Quinn is aware of this work, since he has studied Stillman and his past life. The question that arises here is: Would the detective have read the movements of Stillman as he did, if he had not known about the book? The reader will never know since everything in *The City of Glass* is influenced by chance, but for Quinn, "[k]aum bereit seine 'Leseart' in Frage zu stellen, und weit davon entfernt, Stillmans Motivation und Geisteszustand zu problematisieren, wird die Schrift über der Stadt [...] bedeutungsvoll" (Dallmann 351).

What comes into play is the metaphysical understanding of reality. Interpretation of what the world means to the individual brings reality into existence and this is exactly what Daniel Quinn as Paul Auster does, but at the same time he is not able to process it: "[T]he detective is not so much reading the acts of the pedestrian as he is constructing his own story of the city"(Swope 9). Quinn reads into the story what might lead to a solution of the case, and despite the fact that he has to realize that

---

[13]Here, a connection can be drawn to *Manhattan Transfer* by Dos Passos, because this extratextual reference from the Bible can be found in both novels as a force that will eventually destroy modern New York.

> Stillman had not left his message anywhere. True, he had
> created the letters by the movement of his steps, but they
> have not been written down. It was like drawing a picture
> in the air with your finger. The image vanishes as you are
> making it. There is no result, no trace to mark what you
> have done (Auster 70f.).

Quinn is still not able to understand that he will never be able to end the Stillman case successfully for it lies in the nature of mankind that we want to find a reason for everything in the world. He aptly states: "[N]othing is clear"(40).

There are several other occasions that show that the detective cannot read New York: Firstly, he has difficulties to read and write simultaneously, which results in writing several lines on top of each other, "producing a jumbled, illegible palimpsest" (62). Therefore, his own text of the City becomes unreadable. Secondly, Quinn starts recording and mapping Stillman's movements not until day five, so that the first four letters will never be revealed to him and the reader. Consequently, the text will never be completed. Thirdly, Richard Swope is of the opinion that the message itself, "'THE TOWER OF BABEL', provides 'yet another suggestion of the fragmentation, the unrecoverability, of reality as a text'"(Swope 9). The story of the Tower of Babel explains the variation in human language:

> Go to, let us go down, and there confound their language,
> that they may not understand one another's speech.
> So the Lord scattered them abroad from thence upon the
> face of all the earth: and they left off to build the city.
> Therefore is the name of it called Babel; because the Lord
> did there confound the language of all the earth: and from
> thence did the Lord scatter them abroad upon the face of
> all the earth. ("The King James Bible" Gensis 11:8-9).

The uncountable sum of signs, symbols and languages makes it impossible to understand each other, the world itself becomes fragmented and finally no one has the knowledge about the meaning of his words. New York together with its 'melting pot' citizens are imprisoned in a maze of communication processes that is represented in the City itself, because according to Paul Auster, "New York [is] an inexhaustible place, a labyrinth of endless steps, [...]"(Auster 3).

Moreover, the title of the novel shows that the City of New York is hard to decipher, for *City of Glass* is clearly an ambiguous title. First and foremost, the glassy skyscrapers are a clear sign for the modernity of the City. Mrs. Dallmann explains that "Urbanität [...] bei Auster nicht mehr das Symbol einer spezfischen Lebensweise [ist]: die Welt seiner Erzählungen ist durchgängig urban, es existiert kein ruraler Gegenpol zur Großstadt[14]"(Dallmann 344). Yet, on the one hand, the glassy material is transparent and might be able to reveal the ultimate truth to Quinn and releases him from his questions. According to this interpretation, Quinn might not have been disillusioned and evaluated the search as a "hoax"(Auster 71). On the other hand, glass is also a material that reflects everything in front of it, so that everything is doubled and mirrored. Therefore, "glass also acts as a deterrent, a boundary that forbids access rather than granting it" (Swope 12), thus,knowledge is denied to Quinn.

The result of Quinn's inability to understand that the City is too complex to be read, is a gradual loss of his identity. From the beginning of the story Quinn's place in the world is questioned. He has lost his family, has no friends and lives alone in a small apartment on West 107th Street. Quinn publishes his novel of detective fiction under the pseudonym "William Wilson"[15].

> It was [after his son and wife passed away] that he had taken on the name of William Wilson. Quinn was no longer that part of him that could write books, and although in many ways Quinn continued to exist, he no longer existed for anyone but himself"(Auster 4).

Furthermore, Daniel feels deeply connected to the protagonist of his novels. "It [is] not precisely that Quinn want[s] to be Work, or even to be like him, but it reassure[s] him as he [is] writing his books, to know that he [has] it in him to be Work if he ever chose[s] to be, even if only in his mind"(9). The loss of his family is compensated by taking different identities and as Swope argues, "[a]dd to this 'triad of selves that Quinn had become' his role as Auster [...] it is no wonder Quinn's sense of identity is thrown into crisis"(Swope 2).

This is just the beginning, for Quinn takes on several other identities

---

[14]In *The House of Mirth* Edith Wharton presents such a rural antipole by introducing the country estate of the Dorset family, the "Bellomont".

[15]The name is a reference to the short story *William Wilson* by Edgar Allan Poe.

when observing and talking to Peter Stillman Sr. First, he introduces himself as Daniel Quinn in order to protect the name "Paul Auster" (cf. Auster 74) and not to give himself away as a detective. It seems to be the first time that Quinn identifies himself with his real name, but in fact he is of the opinion that "even the truth, would be an invention, a mask to hide behind and keep him safe" (Auster 74). By introducing himself he also wants to gain Stillman's trust since he prefers not to talk to strangers (cf. Auster 74). On the second meeting with Stillman, Quinn introduces himself as "Henry Dark", because he is a character from a book Stillman once wrote. Third, Daniel Quinn introduces himself as Peter Stillman Jr. in order to provoke emotions in Stillman Sr. and see if he really does not recognize him since they have already met twice. It becomes obvious that each time Quinn meets Stillman, he uses a more provoking identity, first to gain trust, then to access Stillman's mind and finally to trigger an emotional outburst by stepping into his family life.

Over the whole procedure of getting to know the enemy, Quinn does not notice that he starts to lose himself in all those identities he takes on. The next step where he gets rid of yet another part of his already fragmented identity is when he walks the maze of New York himself. Here, to the reader is presented a very factual and unemotional description of the City (cf. Auster 106-108). Street name is ranked after street name and thereby, Paul Auster engages the reader to follow Quinn, just as Quinn has followed Stillman[16].

The time in the alley across the apartment of Stillman Jr. and his wife is another step into selflessness. Quinn does not know how long he has stayed there, because he loses track of time and finally "melt[s] into the walls of the city"(117). When Quinn runs out of money and realizes that he is no longer able to live such a life (cf. Auster 118), he decides to go home to his apartment to West 107th Street. On his way he pauses in front of a shop window and sees himself for the first time after he started to live in the alley. "He [thinks] that he [has] spotted a stranger in the mirror, and in that first moment he turn[s] around sharply to see who it was"(120). He does not recognize himself

---

[16]The reader also tries to read meaning into Quinn's walks and if we map his movements we might see the Tower of Babel, just upside down (cf. Dallmann 364).

anymore, which is another clear indicator that New York is about to steal his identity.

The final step into nothingness is fulfilled when Quinn finds his apartment rented to someone else. "[J]ust as his former name and appearance have slipped from his grasp, the apartment that acted as a spatial anchor for his sense of identity has also vanished"(Swope 6). On entering his former home, he has to realize, "[h]e ha[s] come to the end of himself. He [can] feel it now, as though a great truth ha[s] finally dawned him. There [is] nothing left"(Auster 126).

Finally, Quinn ends up in a "windowless cubicle"(127) of the empty apartment of Stillman Jr., being all naked, his only accompanies are the red notebook and a pen. He starts to write "about the stars, the earth, his hopes for mankind" (131), but soon he has to ask himself "'What will happen when there are no more pages in the red notebook?'" (132). With these words, which are also the last ones in the notebook, Quinn disappears into nothingness, he has literally reduced himself to a point zero. Swope aptly states that "apparently the inexhaustible space of the city proves to be exhaustible after all" (Swope 16).

Quinn's life is ruled by uncertainty, instability, arbitrariness, duplicity and ambiguity. The maze of New York keeps him from reading the signs presented to him correctly. Language, spoken and visualized by Quinn's walking, does not help him in any way since "[n]othing is real except of chance"(Auster 3). There are only fragments left, which bear no meaning at all, so that Quinn and all other characters in the novel become play balls of their own language and eventually drown in the incongruities of the City.

Moreover, Daniel Quinn's wish to restore law and order, which is clearly depicted in his own novels of detective fiction, is parodied by Paul Auster, by making use of the 'anti-detective novel'. First of all, there is no crime since Stillman Sr. never makes any move that would unmask his intentions of killing his son Peter. And secondly, there is no solution to the case since Stillman Sr. commits suicide by jumping from Brooklyn Bridge, Stillman Jr. and his wife disappear. The lack of knowledge leads Quinn into nothingness, he finally loses his identity and vanishes as well.

Therefore, metaphysical New York City becomes a metaphor for an inexhaustible maze, which is exhaustible after all. Fittingly, the final words of this chapter are lent from Paul Auster in order to close the circle : "It made no sense, and because of that, it made all the sense in the world" (294).

4 Conclusion

From the very first day of the founding of the small fur trading settlement by the Dutch in 1614, Nieuw Amsterdam, or since 1664 known as New York, is a fast growing and commercial City which has casted and still casts a spell over people all around the world. The Jeffersonian dream of a virtuous and agrarian society soon had to be given up to make way for the new frontier: the City.

We owe it to the uncountable number of authors who dedicated their works to New York that it became so popular in literature. They were fascinated by its diversity and its continuous motion, because from its first steps as an infant up until today the City is always "becoming". Change can be observed behind every corner in both a physical as well as mental sense and it gives its dwellers the hope of the realization of their dreams. Yet, just as Jefferson's foreshadowed many years earlier, many authors noticed that change can be a bad thing as well for it perverts the people living in the City and corrupts their moral ideals and values:

Surprisingly, all four novels that were analyzed for this thesis reveal New York as a City that disillusions its inhabitants, no matter what their social status is, because neither will their dreams ever become fulfilled nor is there a way to exit this unhealthy environment alive. This is due to the constant and rapid change within the City itself and in the heads of the people which fosters illiteracy and corruption.

Consequently, all metaphors for New York City, although different in their orientation, have quite a negative connotation: Dos Passos' New York becomes a modern Babylon. Everything is fragmented, the scenes he presents to his readers, his characters, the actions of the people, in fact the City itself is now a fragmented place that confuses its dwellers. The reason is provided by the author's own past. As a member of the *Lost Generation*, he can observe a clear development towards greed, capitalism and corruption which will tear New York and its society apart. The city lacks coherence, there is no community anymore, no caring for the fellow man. Everyone is on his own, only interested in becoming richer and gaining more power. Therefore, impersonality and loneliness are the constant companions of the citizens living in the modern metropolis. The face of the City alters so enormously fast that its inhabitants lose track of their lives, they fail to understand what is going on and finally get lost in the jungle of incongruity. They become marionettes in the hand of the puppeteer Manhattan and its tremendous environment.

The New York of Stephen Crane and Edith Wharton can be interpreted as a metaphor for a deterministic life in a cage, whose doors remain closed due to the morally illiterate heroines Maggie Johnson and Lily Bart. Both authors show that the young women are victims of their environment, and are doomed to die since they are not fit enough in a Spencerian way of understanding. Maggie is fooled by the theater and the Church who promote a virtuous and wealthy life far away from Devil's Row. Also the Johnson family can be counted among those who are responsible for her death since they give her a false and unrealistic perception of life and reject her in a time where she could have needed a helping hand. Lily Bart becomes an outcast of society because the *noveaux riches* promote a life that is only ruled by money. Old traditions and values do not count anymore and so Lily becomes isolated and dehumanized by her own folk.

Quite an interesting fact, is that both heroines are always on the move, more exactly on a downward movement, yet each of them in their familiar surrounding. Maggie walks along the streets of New York towards her end, whereas Lily moves from one house to the next until she finally dies. Being on the move is a typical trait for the modern metropolis and becomes even more effective in New York City. The clearly hierarchical structured topography illustrates Maggie's and Lily's path of life.

For a short time Maggie is able to climb the ladder of success, which is mirrored in her job as prostitute in Midtown, but soon she is of no interest anymore and has to descend the latter again and move Downtown until she ends up committing suicide where she has started her life: In the Bowery of New York. Lily Bart, in contrast, constantly moves from her Uptown - dwellings further south. She was on top of the social hierarchy, but her financial circumstances and her loneliness finally force Lily to reside in a boarding house, where she finally dies from an overdose of sedatives.

They are not able to understand the City and its society for they are too innocent and naive to survive in this tremendous environment. The message is clearly of a naturalistic nature, because Stephen Crane and Edith Wharton are both of the opinion that every character is determined by race, milieu and preset ideals. Therefore, neither Maggie nor Lily is able to escape from her cage, which is her environment.

The metaphysical New York of Paul Auster is quite similar to the New York of Dos Passos, even though *City of Glass* was written about seventy years after *Manhattan Transfer* had been published. They both present a City that is fragmented and shed to pieces, so that its inhabitants are not able to clear the jungle of incongruity. The difference between the two is the intention, which is clearly mirrored in the time the novel was written. Whereas Dos Passos wants to draw attention to the growing capitalism and corruption that perverts the citizens, Paul Auster's postmodern New York is already corrupted and tries to show that a fragmented reality cannot be read anymore. The signs become meaningless for now chance rules life. Change is so quick at hand that there is no possibility of constructing a coherent meaning between ones words and reality. The inevitable result is the construction of reality, because mankind always tries to read sense into things, although if there might be no sense at all. Therefore, in a metaphorical way of understanding, New York City in Paul Auster is an inexhaustible maze, which is exhaustible after all, because Quinn fails to understand that the City cannot be understood and finally vanishes altogether.

There are several typical urban traits that can be found in each of the novels and contribute to the negative picture of the City that calls itself 'Center of the Universe'. New York is a constant changing place, nothing ever stays the same, traditions and moral values alter with the consequence that they are wrongly applied (as in the case of Maggie) or get replaced by new rules (as in the case of Lily). The postmodern New York is so broken and subject to chance that Quinn finally has to give up to look for a satisfying answer, because there will never be one.

What follows this machine-like image of the City is isolation and rootlessness. All characters in the novels become lonely at one point in their lives, which then leads to alienation and loss of identity. The City literally dehumanizes its inhabitants, because they are dazzled by its addictive quality beyond recognition.

Despite these negative qualities that seem to represent New York City during the 20th century, it has been and still is the destination for millions of people who dream of a better life in freedom and wealth. Therefore this thesis shall conclude with a more positive outlook by Walt Whitman (1819-1892), one of America's greatest poets. To him New York was more like an ocean, with ever-shifting movements. As already mentioned, each person has to decide what metaphor he connects to the City of New York since there are as many Cities as there are imaginations:

> Ah, what can ever be stately and admirable to me than
> mast-hemm'd Manhattan?
> River and sunset and scallop-edg'd waves of flood-tide?
> The sea-gulls oscillating their bodies, the hay-boat in the
> twilight, and the belated lighter?
> What gods can exceed these that clasp me by the hand,
> and with voices I love call me promptly and loudly
> by my nightest name as I approach?
> What is more subtle than this which ties me to the woman
> or man that looks in my face?
> Which fuses me into you now, and pours my meaning into
> you?
>
> We understand then do we not?
> What I promis'd without mentioning it, have you not
> accepted?
> What he study could not teach - what the preaching could
> not accomplish is accomplish'd, is it not?

(Whitman 143)

5 Appendix

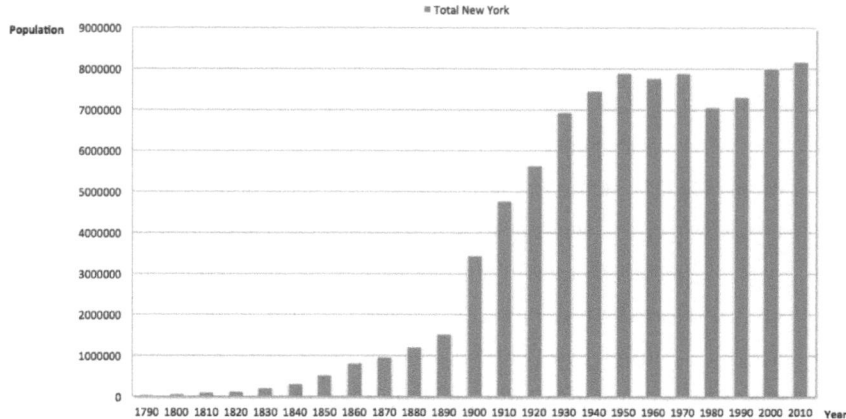

Figure 1: Development of the population of New York City from 1790 - 2010.[17]

---

6 Primary Literature

Auster, Paul. *New York Trilogy: City of Glass*. London: Faber and Faber, 1988.

Crane, Stephen. *Maggie: A Girl of the Streets and Other Tales of New York*. Penguin Classics, 2000.

Jefferson, Thomas. *Notes of the State of Virginia*. Ed. William Peden. Chapel Hill: University of North Carolina Press, 1954.

Passos, John Dos. *Manhattan Transfer*. Boston: Mariner Books, 2000.

Wharton, Edith. *The House of Mirth*. Oxford: Oxford World's Classic, 2008.

Whitman, Walt. "Crossing Brooklyn Ferry". *Writing New York: A Literary Anthology*. Ed. Phillip Lopate. New York: The Library of America, 2008. 143.

7 Secondary Literature

Baldick, Chris, ed. *The Concise Oxford Dictionary of Literary Terms*. Oxford: Oxford University Press, 2001.

Beer, Janet. *Edith Wharton's The House of Mirth*. New York: Routledge Guides to Literature, 2007.

Cf. Herzogenrath, Bernd. *The Art of Desire: Reading Paul Auster*. Amsterdam: Rodopi, 1999.

Dallmann, Antje. *ConspiraCity New York: Großstadtbetrachtung zwischen Paranoia und Selbstermächtigung*. Vol. 176. Heidelberg: Universitätsverlag Winter, 2009. American Studies: A Monograph Series.

Dickstein, Morris. "The City as Text: New York and the American Writer". *TriQuaterly 83* (1991): 183–204.

Flower, Benjamin Orange. "From Civilization's Inferno". *Maggie: A Girl of the Streets. An Authoritative Text, Backgrounds and Sources, the Author and the Novel, Reviews and Criticism*. Ed. Thomas A. Gullason. New York: W.W. Norton & Company, Inc., 1979. 87–89.

Gates, Robert A. *The New York Vision: Interpretations of New York CIty in the American Novel*. Lanham: University Press of America, 1987.

Gelfant, Blanche Housman. "John Dos Passos: The Synoptic Novel". *The American City Novel*. Ed. Blanche Housman Gelfant. Oklahoma: University of Oklahoma Press, 1970. 133–174.

——. "The City Novel as a Literary Genre". *The American City Novel*. Oklahoma: University of Oklahoma Press, 1970. 3–24.

——. "The Destructive Element". *The American City Novel*. Ed. Blanche Housman Gelfant. Oklahoma: University of Oklahoma Press, 1970. 107–119.

Hoffarth, Florian. "Mythos Babylon: Das Konzept von Sprache und Religion in Paul Austers *City of Glass*". *Sic et Non. Zeitschrift für Philosophie und Kutur im Netzt* 5 (2006): 4–12.

Hoffmann, Gerhard. *Raum, Situation, erzählte Wirklichkeit: Poetologische und historische Studien zum englischen und amerikanischen Roman*. Stuttgart: Metzler, 1878.

Ickstadt, Heinz. "Envisioning Metropolis - New York as Seen, Imaged and Imagined. <http://erea.revues.org/1069> (March 24, 2011)". *E-rea* 7.2 (2010): 2–18.

——. "New York und der Stadtroman der amerikanischen Moderne". *Medium Metropole: Berlin, Paris, New York*. Ed. Friedrich Knilli. Heidelberg: Universitätsverlag Winter, 1986. 111–124.

Jackson, Kenneth T. "The Capital of Capitalism: The New York Metropolitan Region, 1890-1940". *Metropolis 1890-1940*. Ed. Anthony Sutcliffe. Chicago: The Universit of Chicago Press, 1984. 319–354.

——. *The Encyclopedia of New York City*. New Haven: Yale University Press, 1995.

Keating, Peter. "The Metropolis in Literature". *Metropolis 1890-1940*. Ed. Anthony Sutcliffe. Chicago: The Universit of Chicago Press, 1984. 129–146.

Kick, Fran. *What Makes Kds KICK: Inspiring the Millennial Generation to KICK IT IN*. Centerville: Instruction & Design Concepts, 2005.

Lopate, Phillip. "Introduction". *Writing New York: A Literary Anthology*. Ed. Phillip Lopate. New York: The Library of America, 2008. XVII –XXII.

Lutwack, Leonard. *The Role of Place in Literature*. Syracuse: Syracuse University Press, 1984.

Oates, Joyce Carol. "Imaginary Cities: America". *Literature and the American Urban Experience: Essays on the City and Literature.* Ed. Michael C. Jaye and Anne Chalmers Watts. Manchester: Manchester University Press, 1981. 11–33.

Pizer, Donald. "Stephen Crane's *Maggie* and American Naturalism". *Maggie: A Girl of the Streets. An Authoritative Text, Backgrounds and Sources, the Author and the Novel, Reviews and Criticism.* Ed. Thomas A. Gullason. New York: W.W. Norton & Company, Inc., 1979. 186–193.

Riis, Jacob A. *How the Other Half Lives: Studies Among the Tenements of New York.* Boston: Bedford Books of St. Martin's Press, 1996.

Salmela, Markku. "New York City as America: Examples from Auster and DeLillo". *How Far is America From Here? Selected Proceedings of the First World Congress of the International American Studies Association, 22-24 May 2003.* Ed. Theo D'haen, et al. New York: Rodopi, 2005. 609–615.

Sauter, Irene Billeter. *New York City: "Gilt Cage" or "Promised Land?" Representations of Urban Space in Edith Wharton an Anzia Yezierska.* Bern: Peter Lang, 2011.

Schaetzle, Jeannine. *The Reflection of the Metropolis in Stephen Crane's Maggie: A Girl of the Streets.* München: Grin, 2000.

Schaller, Hans W. *Der amerikanische Roman des 20. Jahrhunderts.* Leipzig: Ernst Klett, 1998. Uni-Wissen Anglistik, Amerikanistik.

Sorrentino, Paul, ed. *Dictionary of Literary Biography.* Vol. 357. Gale: Cangage Learning, 2010.

Stallman, Robert W. *Stephen Crane: A Biography.* New York: George Braziller, 1968.

Swope, Richard. "Supposing A Space: The Detecting Subject in Paul Auster's *City of Glass*". *Studies Ejournal* 2.3 (2003): MLA International Bibliography.

"The King James Bible". *<http://www.gutenberg.org/dirs/etext05/bib2110h.htm>* (April, 03 2012).

Tygstrup, Frederik. "The Literary City: Between System and Sensation". *Babylon or New Jerusalem? Perceptions of the City in Literature*. Ed. Valeria Tinkler-Villani. New York: Rodopi, 2005. 225–237.

Von der Thüsen, Joachim. "The City as a Metaphor, Metonomy and Symbol". *Babylon or New Jerusalem? Perceptions of the City in Literature*. Ed. Valeria Tinkler-Villani. New York: Rodopi, 2005. 1–11.

Weil, François. "Early Nineteenth-Century New Yorkers and the Invention of New York City. <http://erea.revues.org/1190> (March 24, 2011)". *E-rea* 7.2 (2010): 2–7.

Weimer, David R. *The City as a Metaphor*. New York: Random House, 1966.

Zipris, Lester Roy. "The Lure of the City: Urban Landscape and Metaphor in American Literature, 1870-1920". Diss. State University of New York at Buffalo, 1981.

Zlotnick, Joan. "Skycraper City". *Portrait of an American City: The Novelists' New York*. Port Washington: Kennikat Press, 1982. 87–109.

——. "The Emerging Metropolis". *Portrait of an American City: The Novelists' New York*. Port Washington: Kennikat Press, 1982. 22–47.